let
the
light
pour
in

Also by Lemn Sissay

let
the
light
pour
in

Morning Poems

Lemn Sissay

CANONGATE

First published in Great Britain, the USA and Canada in 2023 by
Canongate Books Ltd,
14 High Street, Edinburgh EH1 1TE

Distributed in the USA by Publishers Group West
and in Canada by Publishers Group Canada

canongate.co.uk

9

British Library Cataloguing-in-Publication Data
A catalogue record for this book is available on
request from the British Library

ISBN 978 1 80530 113 4

Typeset by Palimpsest Book Production Ltd, Falkirk, Stirlingshire

Printed and bound by CPI Group (UK) Ltd, Croydon CR0 4YY

For Ethiopia Alfred

Introduction

Thanks for opening this experiment in hope.

This is how it works. Each morning I take a running leap and I dive into words. I hunt under the surface for the right ones and emerge with the catch. Then I lay them out in a quatrain and press send. Out they go on my socials. I have been doing it for ten years. A daily practice. My meditation. It can take minutes or hours. (Although it rarely actually happens in minutes.)

Time is the DNA of poetry. It can take seconds to read a poem but a lifetime to understand it. It can take a lifetime to write a poem but seconds to understand it. Ask any poet, 'How long does it take to write a poem?' and they will tell you, 'Five minutes or five years'. Equally, the effect of a good poem is that it is timeless. So, taking the pressure of time as an opportunity, why not try to squeeze a lifetime into four lines? Four lines that stay in your mind. Then try again the next morning.

These poems have spread in ways I could not have predicted. Artists have made them into murals on city walls and in art centres. People have them as tattoos. They have comforted the unwell. Women have sung them as dawn breaks in the stone circle at Stonehenge. Cafés have them written on their chalk boards. I'm proud of the journeys they have taken.

I have pored over thousands of them and chosen for you the ones that mean the most. This book is the conclusion of a ten-year dawn project. Morning is the key. A friend advised me to 'Wake with enthusiasm to the dawning of each day'. I like that 'cause when I write I feel like I am opening windows to let the light pour in.

Lemn Sissay, 2023

let
the
light
pour
in

'How do you do it?' said night
'How do you wake up and shine?'
'I keep it simple,' said light
'One day at a time'

Said the mind to the heart
Said the heart to the mind
'The important kind of art
Is the art of being kind'

I am the bull in a China shop
And with all my strength and will
As a storm smashed the teacups
I stood still

Remember you were loved
I felt your spirit grow
I held on for the love of you
And then for love let go

It's all a conversation
Between day and night
Between mist and clarity
Darkness and light

The moon tells the sky
The sky tells the sea
The sea tells the tide
And the tide tells me

Beware the diary of dark frost

The map of black ice and fog

The ink-filled heart uncrossed

The liar's travelogue

Said the sun to the moon
Said the head to the heart
'We have more in common
Than sets us apart'

'I am not defined by darkness'
Confided the night
'At dawn I am reminded
I am defined by light'

I will build an embassy
In your heart over time
There's a plot of land inside me
Build one in mine

Rainbows do it in the car wash
Eyelids do it on eyes
Quasars do it in the cosmos
Make like the sun and rise

I want the sun to be you
And the sky to be me
By the coast and gulls
And rhyming sea

Ecoutez le murmure
De la lune et soleil
À l'aube, ils chantent
'Accueil, accueil'

If someone is copying you
Remember thereupon
Anyone can find the switch
When the lights are on

When darkness comes
To ask of its meaning
Be light upon the shadow
Rise up and lean in

'How do you grow?' said night
'How do you keep it in the day?'
'To keep what I have,' said light
'I have to give it away'

In light of each occasion
Of artist and agent
All representation
Is the art of arrangement

Sleep breaks out, dawn breaks in
A hymn of thunder wakes within
I am the water washed by wind
I am without if not within

I am a lifted kettle, me
I rise and I shine
One cup of tea
And the world is mine

If the phone won't ring, make the call
If the mountain won't move, shift it
If the birds won't sing, sing to them all
And if the sun won't rise, lift it

If I were a desert island
Here's what I'd do
I'd build me a jetty
And wait for you

They have found the abature –
Gripped rips of torn moss –
Lined by spears of silver birch
And a conspiracy of frost

Night exits stage left
Dawn enters stage right
Up stage centre
Write, write, write

A burning procession
In the sky above
Anger is an expression
In search of love

The syllable counters are out again
They wake with their cynical eyes and then
They count all the stresses and shout 'Ahem –
I do so believe there's eleven of them'

Good morning all
Frog's gotta croak
My dawn chorus
'I do not smoke'

Let every fallen shadow
Be surrounded by light
Let dawn unbowed
Emerge from the night

It isn't sunlight
Dawn or the moon
And yet it's
Sun in an Empty Room

It is the last of the part
The end of the start
The heart of the earth
And the end of my heart

In the way light talks to a river
In the way a river holds night beneath
In the way spring calms winter
In this way we should speak

Day breaks
And a split-yolk sun
Oozes on a lightly toasted
And buttered sky

I am gonna creep
Between day and break
Too hot to sleep
Too tired to wake

If it were not imagined
It could not be made
Therefore imagination
Must not be afraid

Grant me serenity
As day breaks from night
Grant my shadows grace
And a cradle of light

We are wildflowers
Wild as the wind
Wild as the dawn
Wild within

Autocorrect Love Poem

I
Live
Yob

Answers like rainfall
In a coffee-bean sky
In my name, I claim all
My name is Why

Spray lifts from the coast
Who loves *truly* lives
Who lives loves most
And most of all, forgives

Ethiopian Airlines
Gold from the stone
Manchester to Addis
Home from home

'I have walked in wilderness,' said night
'With worry pain and righteous ire . . .'
'Put down the cross,' said light
'We need the wood for a fire'

Clouds fall away
In the way they do
Yesterday has gone
I love dew

Remember you were loved
As day loves night, and so
I held you one last time
And then for love let go

Keep it in the day
Even if it's night
Even if it's heavy
Keep it light

Mist surrounds the ship
Icebergs draw near
The crew fall silent
And pray for it to clear

Dawn is a riddle
From the middle of the night
Born in a ripple
In a giggle of light

Evening falls in the arms of day
It does the same each night
The darkest pain fades away
At the gentlest touch of light

Like a paintbrush on canvas
Like each stroke was the last
This is how I will touch you
When all this has passed

The days are longer
They weaken the night
Shadows are stronger
In hunger for light

Alert! I wake and rise from my bed
It is solstice – the light and the way –
And so, 'Welcome dear sun,' I said
And the sun said, 'It was yesterday'

When storms surround me
And surround me they will
I tell myself to bell myself
Hold on and hold still

Moon in a wheelbarrow
Stars in a skip
Dawn holds the handles
Sun gets a grip

Springs wait as evening falls
Dreams hush when night's done
Darkness rests when dawn calls
Windows blush in the sun

Seasonal affective disorder
What hypnotic words to sing
To rise on light and chant
It's spring, it's spring, it's spring

Unrise is sunrise untied from an *s*

Clocks lock without the sea

Team is an anagram of meta

Error is terror without the cup of *t*

My name is Why
It's all I've got
This is my life
In one shot

More than a fleck
Less than a comet
A speck of dust
With bugs upon it

Where are my glasses? Where are my glasses?
My glasses are gone! My glasses are gone!
I've lost my glasses! I've lost my glasses!
. . . I have got my glasses on

Dawn unearths
Gold from the black
The deeper the light
The warmer its back

She left me
And when I wake
My heart like morning
Breaks

Here comes the sun
There goes the night
Words won't wait
Write, write, write!

LET THE LIGHT POUR IN

Open sails
And stretch my spine
The night's gone
The day's mine

The sea and its turbulence
And courage and rage and stress
All the flailing fists will fall
To a gentle coast's caress

The lesson of dawn is
Subtle and sublime –
Take it easy, but take it all
One day at a time

I stand in light perfectly still
A shadow moved then hid
I've no more than what I saw
I've nothing to prove it did

'What did I witness last night?'
Said a shocked and bowing moon
'We must stand up for light'
Said the sun, 'and soon'

Let each drop let each droplet
Each drop let each droplet
Each drop let each drop
Let each drop let each droplet

White queen takes black bishop
Black rook moves two down
White bishop bristles

Dawn takes night

Surf the tidal wave from night
Onto the shore of the day
Then walk like a champion
To the beach café

Dawn is the spell-checker
For the dreams of night
They cast their spells in the dark
And wait by the sea for light

Today, no thrashing seas
No frightened birds, no storm
I'm the guy that lives in
A lighthouse at dawn

Again: night meets a new day
This time above the ocean
'It's like speed dating,' said the sea
'In slow motion'

And so, embattled revolutionary
And grand king of the throne
Who will free this shadow
From this stone?

How weak the night lies
As light aerates the dark
And atomic dreams multiply
From a graphene heart

There is a hole in the sky
Where light falls through
Where the whole of me
Is the whole of you

'How do you do it?' said night
'How do you wake and sing?'
'I surround shadows,' said light
'People, places and things'

Crack the dawn awake
Break the tide of grief
Tide and time won't wait
Water rushes beneath

As the sun ripens at dawn
I type the light and try
To reach through the day
And pluck it from the sky

Raise me with sunrise
Bathe me with light
Kiss all the shadows
That fell from the night

Then came October
Winter's first kiss
The frost upon
Summer's lips

I stopped fighting for a second
A shadow boxer frozen in time
All I have is all there is
And this little light of mine

The boy with a stone in his fist
Stands at the bank of the lake
The sun rises, the stone drops
Wait, wait, wait

'I'm tired,' said the moon
'I'm heavy with night'
'Keep it simple,' said the sun
'And light'

There's much I've done
There's much to do
But I'm undone
When it comes to you

The girl with a stone in her fist
Stood by the bank of the lake
She closed her eyes and made a wish
And opened her fist to fate

I walk through doors backwards
To keep my eye on the light
'I do the same,' said the day
'To night'

At dawn – a wake for dusk –
Light will find what it must –
What will be will be – thus
Shadows speak for us

I'll not get in the way of things
Sun weaves light in a loom
I wake with cloth wings
By light and the morning moon

My roots twisted far away
From the family tree
I searched forests to find her
To ask if she would find me

Fetch wood, carry water
Look after your back
It ain't where you go
It's where you're at

Love is part spell, part curse
Each night by stars or storm
She waits on the edge of earth
For a glimpse of him at dawn

Frank, incensed, shouted
'Star!' he said, 'Star!
I couldav got me satnav
From the boot of the car'

A shoal of stars in ocean night
Moon adrift with cargo light
Captain yawns, 'Dawn's in sight –
All is well, all is right'

'How do you hold on,' said night
'To peace in the day?'
'To keep what I have,' said light
'I have to give it away'

Each time you go
Part of me hates you
It's not you though
It's the loss I relate to

How darkness runs
From fading shade
How bright the sun
How unafraid

Sun rises red
Sky is blue
Even my silhouette
Misses you

What is there without you?
What seeds unsown?
What will not spring?
What is left unknown?

I will run
Coast to coast –
In sight to some
Unknown to most

To unrise is to sleep
To unhand unrest
Unless it's sunrise
Uncoupled from an *s*

'Save it for now!'
Said day to night
'Say what needs to be said
When the time is right'

I stand on bridges at sunrise
And bathe in the laughter of light
Shadow falls behind me
And that's all right

We R older
We are wiser
And we still
Like TIZER!

The sun is apostrophe
The moon is too
Yesterday is lost to me
Today is 'you'

Goodness grows for those that know
To bloom is to know your roots
To give earth all it's worth
Tend to the new shoots

Do the day thing
Do the night thing
Do the play thing
Do the right thing

A pause between end and applause
The Valkyrie's delight
A graceful bow from darkness
And a standing ovation of light

If you don't do it today
There will be no end
Decompress the stress
And then press send

Waves break on the beach's back
Gulls escape the sky
Dawn wades through peaceful black
Night waves goodbye

Raise me with sunrise
Bathe me with light
Kiss all the shadows
That fell from the night

So I opened them
The curtains and page
Light flooded in
And out the rage

Here is where night fell
Where the shadow stood
Yet here comes the light swell
Of blameless likelihood

Night can't drive out night
Only the light above
Fear can't drive out fear
Only love

With a glowing harpoon
She shot the sky at night
Dawn is the boy
With the moon for a kite

Dawn's dragoons
Charge on night
And storm the moon
With swords of light

Politics does not own
Words, the sky or you
If you flew the nest
You are an immigrant too

Night drifts from the dock
With a light wind in its sails
I sit sunlit upon a rock
And hear the hymn of whales

In that space between want and wish
The gap betwixt a dream and myth
Above the sea below mist
The you, the me, the kiss

Just to know you'd call
To tell you where I've been
To be your star above all
To be your sunlit dream

The moon can't forget
How the stars were born
She walks half the earth
For a glimpse of you at dawn

I remember the sunrise
The day after you left
The falling cloak of mist
The roiling regret

Be my Easter Rising
Be my imperfection
Be my peace talks
My rebel insurrection

Never cook
In a bad mood
All that energy
Goes into the food

Rise, rise from out your bed
There are dreams in the air
Harvest light for days ahead
And shine it everywhere

The sun rises at long last
And fills the sky above
Without fear or favour
It is a labour of love

The day's the play
The sun's the star
The sky's the script
I learn it by heart

Translation depending
On the language of the heart
The darker the ending
The lighter the start

Above the orange grove
Under a clementine sky
A low mirabelle sun
On a pomegranate high

'You are my only family,'
Said the sun to the moon
'How did it get so late
So soon?'

She's gone. She left while I was away.
All pre-agreed. I'm in fine fettle.
She took the WiFi, but worst of all
She took the bloody kettle!

I dance on bridges at sunrise
And bathe in the laughter of light
A shadow falls behind me
And that's all right

'Not lost,' said the sun
At the start of the day
'Just following the sky
And finding my way'

'We don't talk enough,'
Said the sun to the moon
'We have too little time
And too much room'

At last I can say it
Out in the open air
I'm so happy I'm here
And you're over there

What was taken from me I'll use
To create a new home
The stone the builder refused
Will be the head cornerstone

I love sleeping in a tent
I love the sound of morning rain
I love tea with good friends
Summer's back again

LEMN SISSAY

We have lived under a thousand skies
We are merely its passing guests –
A twinkle in our parents' eyes –
Born in the NHS

140

This little island
With its little angry people
And its little shouty church
And its pointy little steeple

Leave alone the heartless
Landlords of decay
Light breaches darkness
Every single day

'Stop screaming!' shouted the moon
'Stop shouting!' screamed the night
'I'm leaving,' said the moon
'Stay,' said light

Guide me with your light
Take me through today
I'm tired and losing sight
Might you light the way?

Meet me by the morning
On the corner of night
Where mist rises
And hope's in sight

If you're accused of being a persecutor
By a 'friend' who said you saved her
Karpman's Drama Triangle
May explain the friend's behaviour

Last night I had a nightmare
Imprisoned by my clone
I watched him tap the screen
I was trapped inside his phone

It might come as a shock to you
So hold tight and hold steady
I know you think you've a lot to do
But I'm afraid you peaked already

Then came November
Winter's second kiss
Wind blows tender – cold
Descends upon her lips

Let's be vapour trails
Across the skyline
I cross your mind
You cross mine

Give my body wings
Give me them at night
So I can rise again
In a democracy of light

I'm drawn to the feed
Like a pig to the trough
And I read, and I read
Turn it off, turn it off

Lines don't end with 'with'
Nor with an ampersand
Nor 'nor' nor 'is' nor 'for'
And neither with an 'and'

Sunrise or sunset
Prose or poem
It doesn't matter
Keep going, keep going

Mist lies on quiet crops
And sleeps on the hill
Sunlight rests on clifftops
And everything is still

This isolation is connecting us all
The lake was reflecting the moon
This isolation is collecting us all
Like *Sun in an Empty Room*

The workshop on spoonerism
In a china shop was overlooked
It said on the door outside the room
'Fully booked'

LEMN SISSAY

'About time,' said night
'I've been waiting for you'
'One day at a time . . .' said light
'. . . Is all I can do'

Batman: To the bat cave
Robin: Really . . .? Now?
Batman: Thwack
Robin: Ow

A quiet sailor of words
With subtle ways to be
Named his yacht
The Silent Sea

I am a visible original
A pinnacle of miracle
Critical untypical and
All but inexplicable

My friend is 'Wheresme'
She marries quite a lot
She divorced Mr Keys
And wedded Mr Sock

Spring waits as evening falls
Dreams hush when it's done
Night rests then dawn calls
And windows rush to the sun

'Michael Rosen knows the laws'
The thoughtful word doctor said
The nurse whispered like in *Jaws*
'We're gonna need a bigger bed'

I have seen your greatness
The strength of your will
What it took you to get this far
Is what will take you further still

With a cautious eye
She heard the cry of morning
So she lifted the lid off the sky
And let the light pour in

Named by ripples
Praised by light
Dawn is day's child
Delivered by night

Caught in a safe
A voice shouted 'Halt!'
I realised there and then
It was not my vault

Just because the majority do it
Doesn't mean that it is right
Most of us call it a blue tick
But it isn't blue, it's white

Let's fall apart together
Said darkness to light
Tumbling into sunrise
And out of sight

A toffee-apple dawn
A candy-floss coast
A sugared-orange sun
On marmalade toast

To unwind he unpicked the thread
Got up and unmade the bed
He undrew the curtains and, uncertain,
Left what was untold unsaid

Like a shadow in the wind
A brief reflection on glass
Like a wave beneath a wing
This too shall pass

A molten eagle (whose gold eye
Emboldened a woodland of mist)
Dived from the sage and honey sky
And scooped up the night in its fist

This rising sun
This earth and light
This is my Ethiopia
My birth and my right

Be upside down
And inside out
Go the wrong way round
A roundabout

Be my spring in Budapest
Be my Jo'burg storm
Be my heatwave in Awassa
My African dawn